Today I Made My
First Communion

Written by
Dianne Ahern

Illustrated by
Bill Shurtliff

Published by Aunt Dee's Attic

Today I Made My First Communion
Revised Edition

Published by Aunt Dee's Attic, Inc.
3361 North Maple Road
Ann Arbor, MI 48105

Manufactured in Italy by L.E.G.O. SpA
December 2011

Printed with Ecclesiastical Permission. Most Reverend Earl Boyea, February 8, 2010.

Rescript: In accord with canon 827, S3 of the *Code of Canon Law,* and after having received a *votum* of the *censor librorum,* Msgr. George C. Michalek, permission is granted to publish TODAY I RECEIVED MY FIRST COMMUNION, Revised Edition, by Dianne Ahern. The work is spiritual reflection on the first reception of Holy Eucharist. Given in the Curia of the Diocese of Lansing on this the 2nd day of February, 2010.

By order of the Most Reverend Bishop Earl Boyea
Bishop of Lansing
February 2, 2010

Nihil Obstat: Rev. Msgr. Sylvester I. Fedewa, S.T.L., D.Min.
Censor Librorum—First Edition

Imprimatur: Most Reverend Carl F. Mengeling
Bishop of Lansing
November 9, 2004—First Edition

Library of Congress Control Number: 2009944146

ISBN-13: 978-0-9679437-6-3

3 4 5 6 7 8 9 10 11 12

www.auntdeesattic.com

Dedication

This book is dedicated to my brother, Michael.
Thanks for going first and letting me know it's okay.

Acknowledgments

A very special thank you to all the wonderful people who helped make this book possible, especially:

- The Reverend Father Roger Prokop (RIP), former Pastor of St. Thomas the Apostle Catholic Church, and the original inspiration and model for Father Hugo.

- The Reverend Father William Ashbaugh, current Pastor of St. Thomas the Apostle Catholic Church, and the current Father Hugo inspiration and model.

- All the people who inspired, pre-read, and provided comments and advice, including members of the Shurtliff family, Kristin Bos, Leo DiGiulio, Christie McGuire, Elizabeth Solsburg, Shiobhan Kelly, and the Bishop's Office of the Diocese of Lansing.

- Jillian Downey, text designer and layout artist.

- Mrs. McGuire's second grade class at St. Thomas the Apostle School.

CHAPTER 1
First Communion Class

The big heavy doors swung open, giving up a squeak. Maria and Riley peeked inside. They had both been to church hundreds of times before, but always with their families. This time was different. They were entering on their own, on their way to the first class to prepare for their First Holy Communion.

Riley stumbled forward, pushing Maria through the door. Squeak. Click. The door shut behind them. Suddenly it went from daylight to near dark.

As their eyes adjusted, they could see a second set of doors. These were swinging doors. "This is scary," Maria confessed.

"Oh, we'll be all right," said Riley with not a lot of confidence. "Here's the holy water. Let's bless ourselves."

They did a quick dip of their fingers and a fast, 'In the name of the Father, the Son, and the Holy Spirit. Amen'.

As they opened the second set of doors they could immediately sense a change from the outside world. The air in the church was sweet smelling. It made their skin feel damp and slightly cool, yet comfortable, like a soft blanket.

"Mommy says you can smell the saints praying when you go into a church," whispered Maria. "I think I can feel them, too!"

Suddenly they could see a bright light shining in the area of the altar. It fell upon the figure of Christ hanging on the cross. They just stood there for a moment, fascinated by the cross, but not knowing exactly why. Then, just below the cross, in the front pews, they could see Father Hugo with a group of children and a lady, Ms. Kelly. They rushed forward to be with them.

"Welcome, Maria and Riley. Please come and sit here in front of me. I think you are the last two members of this year's First Communion class to arrive," said Father Hugo. "Shall we get started?" he asked.

Suddenly Father knelt down. The children followed his lead and scooted off the pews and onto their knees. Father led them in the Sign of the Cross, an Our Father prayer, and a joyful Amen! He stood and smiled as the children settled back in the pews.

Father Hugo told the class that for the next 12 weeks they would be meeting here in the church or in the parish hall at 9 o'clock on Saturday mornings. Ms. Kelly, the Director of Religious Education, would be their teacher. Before they could make their First Communion, the children would have to study their prayers, prepare for First Reconciliation, and learn what happens in the Mass. Some Saturdays, he explained, Sister Mary Rose would join them to practice the songs they should know for their First Communion day Mass. Deacon Paul would help them with their prayers.

"Children," Father said most proudly. "This is a very important time in your life. You are about to learn about the Mystery of the Eucharist!"

"Mystery of the Eucharist," whispered Maria to Riley. "I love mysteries. My older brother, Luca, is always reading mystery stories to me."

"Do you know how to solve a mystery?" asked Riley in a low voice.

"Maybe," said Maria, her eyes growing big and dark like jumbo black olives.

Before she could say another word, both Maria and Riley felt the presence of Father Hugo standing over them.

"What is so important that the two of you have to whisper in my class?" questioned Father Hugo.

Maria swallowed hard, trying to get a lump out of her throat. "Father," she said, "if you let us try, I think Riley and I can solve the Mystery of the Eucharist."

Suddenly Riley felt like his whole body was on fire. All he wanted to do was to hide under the pew. He and Maria were next door neighbors and had been best friends practically their entire lives. They often played tricks on their parents and got in and out of jams together, but somehow solving a mystery together, especially one called the Eucharist, seemed much too much. What was she thinking?!

"You want to solve the Mystery of the Eucharist?" said a surprised and somewhat befuddled Father Hugo. He squinted and frowned as he looked back and forth at Maria and Riley. The expression on his face turned from serious to thoughtful and finally to smiling.

"Well, I guess we could let you try," he said looking at Ms. Kelly and rubbing his chin. "I have to admit that the lessons you are about to learn will lead you to the Mystery of the Eucharist.

"Let's give it a shot. Class, are you willing to help Maria and Riley with this mission?"

The other children's responses were mixed. Some seemed confused, others doubtful, but the majority were excited and enthusiastic.

"Children," Father Hugo went on. "This church is filled with clues about the mystery of Jesus' life, the Holy Trinity, and the Eucharist. Between now and next Saturday I want each of you to spend time in the church. Feel free to walk around and look at everything. Pick out something you think might be a 'clue' to solving the mystery or that you find really interesting. We will discuss your clues in upcoming classes."

This made all the children sit up and take notice. Some giggled; others whispered. Getting ready for First Communion was going to be FUN!

"However," beamed Father Hugo, "this does not mean that you do not have to study the lessons in your First Communion workbook."

The rest of the morning was spent with Ms. Kelly learning about things like why God made us, the first man and woman, Adam and Eve, and what happened when they disobeyed God, and how God sent his Son, Jesus, to teach us about love and how to get to heaven.

The next day was Sunday. Maria was up early and was very anxious to go to early Mass. This surprised her father because, of all his children, Maria was always the last one to get up on Sunday. "Maria, why are you up so early?" asked her father.

"Daddy, I want to get to church early today so that I can look for clues to solve the Mystery of the Eucharist!"

Her father gave her a puzzled look. He began to wonder just what was she learning in her First Communion class.

As they entered the church, Maria noticed a lot of people already in the church. They were all talking out loud and in a kind of harmony. Maria listened for a while then asked her father what they were doing. He said, "They are praying the rosary to Mary, the Mother of God."

"I don't understand. What's that mean?" Maria asked in a loud whisper. Could this be a clue to the Mystery of the Eucharist she wondered?

"Well," her father said, "it's a little difficult to explain it all to you right here and right now. Let's just listen and pray along with them. You know the prayers, mostly the Our Father and Hail Mary. After Mass you can ask Aunt Isabella about it. I think she is the best one to explain the mysteries of the rosary to you."

Mysteries of the rosary? More mysteries! Maria frowned. That lump was back in her throat. Going to Aunt Isabella's house for her Sunday visit was going to have added importance today.

After Mass Father Hugo could see the children from the First Communion class walking around the church and looking at things. This is going to be very interesting, he thought to himself with a sense of satisfaction and amazement.

CHAPTER 2
Inside Our Church

The next Saturday, Maria and Riley were really looking forward to their First Communion class. What clues, they wondered, would be uncovered to help them solve the Mystery of the Eucharist?

"Good morning children," began Father Hugo with a twinkle in his eye. "Before Ms. Kelly joins us for your lesson, we have some unfinished business. I want to hear your questions about the Church and see if I can help you solve the Mystery of the Eucharist. Who wants to be first?"

All the hands shot up in a flash. "Good," said Father Hugo. "Maria, since you and Riley started all this business about solving the mystery, let's start with you."

"Father," Maria began, "last Sunday before Mass I heard a lot of people talking in church. My dad said they were praying the rosary. In the afternoon I asked my Aunt Isabella about it. She said that the rosary is a set of prayers said on beads and when we pray it we ask Mary to pray to God to help us.

"Aunt Isabella says the rosary is divided into mysteries; joyful, sorrowful, glorious, and luminous mysteries. She said the mysteries of the rosary relate to special times in Jesus' and Mary's lives that we wouldn't know about unless God revealed them to us."

"Very good, Maria. That is an excellent explanation of the 'mysteries' of the rosary."

As Father continued talking, Maria tried to make a connection between the mysteries of the rosary and the Mystery of the Eucharist, and how God reveals things to us. She thought hard and long, but was too shy to ask another question.

"Riley, what is your question about the church?" asked Father Hugo.

"Father Hugo, why is there holy water near all church doors and why do we cross ourselves when we enter and leave the church?" asked Riley.

"Excellent question! Remember, Riley, last year when your baby sister Delaney was baptized. I poured water over her forehead and said, 'I baptize you in the name of the Father, and of the Son, and of the Holy Spirit'. I told you then that baptism made her a member of our Church and of Christ and gave her special protection from evil. Well, each time you dip your fingers into the holy water and make the Sign of the Cross, you are remembering your own baptism," explained Father Hugo.

"Whoa!" said Riley. "That's pretty special." He wasn't absolutely sure, but Riley thought that the Father, Son, and Holy Spirit had something to do with the Mystery of the Eucharist.

"Now, who else has a question about the church?" asked Father Hugo.

"What are all the pictures on the walls around the church about, Father?" asked T.J. (short for Timothy Joseph).

"Ah-umm. Why do churches have colored windows?" asked Marisa.

"Why is there a table up there?" questioned Ryan pointing to the sanctuary.

"What's inside that big gold box?" asked Matthew pointing to the tabernacle.

"What's behind that door?" asked Andrew pointing to the door to the reconciliation room at the back of the church.

"What's behind those doors up there?" asked Mary Carol pointing to the doors on each side of the altar that lead to the sacristy.

"How come there is an 'eye' on that window? It's looking right at me!" exclaimed Giancarlo pointing to a stained glass window.

"I want to know why you use candles in church instead of light bulbs? Light bulbs are safer," advised Nadine.

"Father, why do you burn that smelly stuff in the little pot on a chain in church sometimes?" questioned Yasmine holding her nose ever so politely.

"Why do we have to be quiet in church?" asked Bridget.

"And how come people sing out loud?" questioned her twin sister Erin. "Some people sing really loud and squeaky!" she complained. The class laughed.

"How come that place where you baptize the babies is so big?" Danny wanted to know.

"What's in that cabinet over there on the wall?" asked Anthony.

"Romano and I went up there last week," said Enrico pointing to the choir loft. "Our dad showed us the big organ pipes; some of them are bigger than us!"

"My, my. You certainly are a curious bunch of children, aren't you? You have some very, very good questions. I mean clues!" commented Father Hugo.

"If you look in the back of your books, children, you will find A MAP OF OUR CHURCH that shows the names, places, and an explanation of the things you just asked about."

"You know," he said, "one very nice thing about the Catholic Church is that you will find these very same items in each and every church throughout the world. They may be in slightly different arrangement, and sometimes you may have to look to find them, but they will be there."

"Let us take a walk around the church, and I will answer some of your questions as we go. You know, Maria and Riley, these questions provide excellent clues to the Mystery of the Eucharist," said Father Hugo with a mischievous grin on his face.

The children clamored out of the pews, and hurried to follow Father Hugo. Down the aisle they scrambled, running to keep up with him.

"Stand here and just look around you," said Father Hugo mid-way down the aisle. "Look at our beautiful church." The children's eyes widened as they whirled around taking in the sights.

"See the altar, that's the table that Ryan asked about," said Father. "It's elevated to emphasize the absolute importance of everything that takes place on the altar. That's where God changes bread and wine into the Body and Blood of Jesus in the Eucharistic sacrifice!"

Maria and Riley's ears prickled and the skin on their arms got goose bumps hearing the words 'Eucharistic sacrifice'.

"Look right behind the altar. See the big gold box that Matthew asked about? It's called the 'tabernacle'. It's the place where we place the consecrated bread after Communion. The consecrated bread is the Eucharist, the Body of Christ. It waits there until it can be given in Communion at a later service or until either Deacon Paul or a lay minister or I can take it to parish members who are in nursing homes, hospitals, or who cannot come to Mass because they are sick."

"There is a candle burning beside the tabernacle. That candle is always lit when the Eucharist is in the tabernacle. The candle lets us know that Christ is present and re-

minds us to show reverence by being quiet and bowing or genuflecting before Him."

"Nadine, you wanted to know why we use candles instead of light bulbs. Well, you know God sent Jesus into the world to set the world on fire for us! To light up our lives with His love! To show us the way to the truth," said Father with passion in his voice. "You just cannot do that with a light bulb, now can you, Nadine?"

"No, Father Hugo, you sure can't," said Nadine in her shy voice.

As they walked further down the aisle, Father called their attention to the stained glass windows. "Look at these beautiful windows," exclaimed Father Hugo.

"The stained glass windows in churches often tell stories about our faith. See those three over the altar. They tell the stories of Jesus' birth, death, and resurrection. The first one is of Jesus, Mary, and Joseph at the birth of Jesus in the stable in Bethlehem. You all know that story I hope! It was Christmas day; God became man and dwelt among us!

"The middle window shows Jesus dying on the cross. Beneath Him are His mother, Mary, and friends John and Mary of Magdala.

"The third window shows Jesus raised from the dead. That's our mystery of faith right there," stated Father Hugo. "Jesus, God-became-man, died for our sins so that we might be forgiven. Then He rose from the dead and ascended to heaven where He sits at the right hand of the Father. Out of love He sent the Holy Spirit, the Third person in the Trinity, to guide us. Oh my!"

Father seemed as if he were in deep prayer as he gazed at the windows. Maria and Riley, hearing the word 'mystery' again, looked at each other and wondered.

"Look at all the stained glass windows along the sides of the church," directed Father Hugo. "Notice that they are all similar, except each one has a different symbol near the top. Each symbol reminds us of a different aspect of our faith.

"That 'eye in the triangle' that Giancarlo asked about is the 'all-seeing eye of God'. Remember last week in class Ms. Kelly taught you that God is everywhere and sees everything. Well, that 'eye' reminds us of this. The triangle around the eye reminds us of the three persons in God. Who are the three persons of God?" Father asked the class.

"The Father, the Son, and the Holy Spirit," recited the class in unison.

"Correct!" said Father. "This has to be the smartest First Communion class ever," he stated with pride.

"Look at these three windows, children. The lamb, the wheat, and the grapes. Now these are real clues to the Mystery of the Eucharist!" declared Father Hugo.

"You see the lamb. That represents the Lamb of God. Jesus, the Son of God, given to us in the Eucharist, is the Lamb of God."

"Let me tell you a story," said Father Hugo. "Throughout history, people have always wanted to make sacrifices to God in order to gain His favor or forgiveness, and to glorify Him. The lamb was one of the most frequently sacrificed animals in ancient, Jewish rituals. In biblical times people would bring their animals to the Temple in Jerusalem where the priest would perform the sacrifice as an offering to God. There were lots of rules regarding how the animals would be killed and what would be done with their blood and meat. The animal's blood was thought to be the life force. The Jews believed the animal's blood given in sacrifice could help them get rid of sins and weaknesses that separated them from God. However, the animal blood had no life power and, despite the sacrifices, the people typically continued in their sinful ways.

"We know from the Bible that one day John the Baptist saw Jesus walking toward him and he said, 'Behold, the Lamb of God' (John 1:29, 36). John recognized Jesus as the Messiah and knew that He was the one

who had come to save the world. As you will learn more about later, in the end Jesus shed His blood on the cross as a sacrifice and in atonement for the sins of humankind. That is so that our sins could be forgiven and we could be united with God in heaven. Jesus became the Sacrificial Lamb, the Lamb of God."

"But Father, that lamb in the window doesn't look dead," observed Danny.

"That's right!" said Father Hugo. "That is because Jesus, The Lamb of God, rose from the dead."

"Wow! That's a great story. What about the wheat and grapes?" asked Riley.

"The wheat," continued Father Hugo, "begins as a tiny grain or seed that is put in the soil, and through a miracle it germinates and grows to a mature plant using the earth, sun, and rain. When the wheat is fully grown the grain is harvested, milled, and made into bread. We all know that bread is a basic food that we must have to nourish our earthly bodies. In a very special way, in the celebration of the Eucharist at Mass, Jesus becomes the bread for our spiritual body, our soul, promising us eternal life if we follow Him."

"Grapes, like wheat, are fruits of the earth, and grow on vines. Grapes are used to produce wine. Throughout the Bible, Jesus uses vines and grapes and wine to describe our relationship with God. At the Last Supper, Jesus gave the Apostles His own blood under the form of wine and promised them that drinking His blood would bring them forgiveness of sins and eternal life. This too is part of the Eucharistic celebration."

"Whew!" exclaimed Maria. "They drank His blood? That sounds perfectly disgusting!"

"Oh, no, Maria. It is really the most beautiful thing in the entire world. You see, the wine becomes the blood of Jesus through the action of the Holy Spirit when the priest prays over it. The blood of Jesus still looks and tastes like wine. However, our faith tells us that it is no longer just wine, but rather the blood of the Eternal Son of God, Jesus Christ, the Second Person of the Holy Trinity. You will learn more about all this in a few weeks when we study the Mass."

As they began to walk back toward the front of the Church, Father Hugo pointed out the pictures that line the walls that T.J. had asked about called the Stations of the Cross.

"The Stations of the Cross tell the story of how Jesus was put to death. How He was sacrificed. There are fourteen stations in all. You will learn more about the Stations and what they represent when you are a little older. But let's today walk through them because they are so very important.

"They begin with Jesus being condemned to die. Next he is sent to Pontius Pilate who had Jesus scourged—which is a very cruel form of punishment. Then the Roman soldiers mocked Him. They put a crown of thorns on his head and called Him 'King of the Jews'.

"Jesus was made to carry the cross on which He would be nailed. He carried it through the streets of Jerusalem to Calvary, the place outside the walled city of Jerusalem where Roman soldiers put criminals to death. Along the way He fell three times under the weight of the cross. A woman stepped out of the crowd to wipe the sweat and blood from His face. Then a man helped Him to carry the cross for a while. When Jesus got to Calvary, tired and bleeding, they nailed Him to that cross. After hanging on the cross for three long hours, Jesus gave up His spirit to God the Father; He died. Later His friends took His body down from the cross and laid it in a new tomb. That is how they buried people back then."

"Do you know what happened next, children?" asked Father Hugo in a whisper of suspense. The children were leaning forward to hear the ending of the best story ever told.

"He rose from the dead on Easter Morning! Alleluia!" shouted Father Hugo as he swung his arms up into a big 'V', making the children gasp and laugh in relief.

"Do you know what good news this is!?" Father continued. "It means that Jesus had won the victory over death—not only His death but the death of everybody who believes in Him. It also means that, in the end, good always triumphs over evil!

"That's all the stories we have time for now, children," said Father Hugo. "We will talk about the other things in the church on another day. But do look in the back of your books to see a diagram of the church and read the descriptions of the things found in our church."

As Maria and Riley walked back toward the front of the church, they seemed bewildered. Surely they had received a lot of clues about the Mystery of the Eucharist. But were they any closer to solving it?

CHAPTER 3
Praying with Deacon Paul

Good Morning class. My name is Deacon Paul. Ms. Kelly invited me to talk to you about prayer. Now, who can tell me why we pray?" asked Deacon Paul.

All the hands shot up as each child was sure he or she knew the answer to this question. Some of the responses Deacon Paul heard were:

"To thank God for our mommy and daddy, and to thank God that daddy has a good job," said Marisa.

"To ask God to help me stay out of trouble," quipped Riley.

"To ask God to help my grandpa get well," said Danny.

"We say a prayer to thank God for our food before we have dinner," said Bridget.

"Sometimes we say the rosary in the car so that we will have a safe trip," offered Nadine.

"All very good answers," commented Deacon Paul. "We use prayer to get closer to God and to talk to God, don't we? Often we recite prayers that we have memorized and know that God likes to hear. Some of the favorites are the Our Father, the Hail Mary, and the Glory Be. Sometimes, however, we just make up our own prayers.

"When we pray we sometimes ask God for things, sometimes we give Him thanks and praise, sometimes we even make promises to God in our prayers. What else do we do in our prayers?" questioned Deacon Paul.

This time there weren't any hands waving, but Deacon Paul could see by the looks on their faces that the children were all thinking very hard.

"Don't we listen to God, too?" he asked the children. The children nodded their heads and a quiet chorus of "yes" could be heard.

"Correct," he assured them. "When we ask God to help us to be good and to help us with a problem, we have to listen for His answer. He answers us through our hearts, our minds, and our consciences. If we open our hearts to God, He will always send us in the right direction. We can always trust God!"

Deacon Paul continued, "We also have to understand that sometimes God doesn't answer our prayers right away, and sometimes He doesn't give us the answer we want to hear. For instance, Danny knows that it seems like God is pretty slow in answering his prayers for his grandpa to get better. He has been sick for a long time, hasn't he Danny? Danny also knows that God just may not make his grandpa well here on earth. God may prefer that his grandpa go to heaven to get better and to be free of his illness. And we have to accept that as 'God's will'."

"Who has heard the phrase, 'God's will be done on earth as it is in heaven'?" questioned Deacon Paul.

"I think it is part of the Our Father," offered Maria.

"That's right, Maria. Children, do you know that even Jesus prayed to God? One time the Apostles saw Jesus praying, and they asked Him to teach them how to pray, too. That's when Jesus taught the Apostles to pray the Our Father! You'll find the story of this in your Bibles in Matthew 6:9-13 and also in Luke 11:2-4.

"Children, please turn to the back of your books, to the section that says PRAYERS I SHOULD KNOW. Let's all read the Our Father together," instructed Deacon Paul. "It is the best prayer we can say."

After they recited the Our Father, they read the other prayers in the back of the book and discussed their meaning.

Deacon Paul gave them an assignment. They were to practice reading out loud and try to memorize the words to the Sign of the Cross, the Our Father, the Hail Mary, and the Apostles' Creed. He also asked them to review the Commandments. They learned about the Commandments when they studied the Sacrament of Penance and Reconciliation so this would just be a refresher.

"Can you do that?" he asked. They nodded yes. "Oh, and another assignment. When you go to Mass tomorrow, listen carefully to Father Hugo and see if you hear some familiar prayers said during Mass."

After class was over, Maria and Riley sat on the steps in front of the church. Riley opened his book to the prayers and read the Apostles' Creed out loud to Maria. "Maria! Remember when Father Hugo was looking at the stained glass windows over the altar and he said how Jesus was born, died, and rose from the dead, and that was the Mystery of our Faith. Well, this Apostles' Creed talks about that, too. Do you think it is related to the Mystery of the Eucharist?"

"It has to be," said Maria with certainty. "But I just haven't figured it out yet."

As they were sitting in front of the church, Sister Mary Rose, the music minister, was walking by and stopped when she came to where they were.

"My, my. You two look lost in your thoughts. Can I help?" offered Sister Mary Rose.

"Deacon Paul was just helping us with our prayers. I am getting pretty confused now, especially about all the mysteries," admitted Maria.

"Yes, Sister," explained Riley. "Maria and I told Father Hugo we would solve the Mystery of the Eucharist, and I don't think we are getting very far."

"Solving the Mystery of the Eucharist. I'd say that is a pretty big assignment!" said a surprised Sister Mary Rose.

"When I have a problem to solve, I always pray to God for help. Maybe I can help you with a prayer," offered Sister Mary Rose as she sat down beside them. "Let me see if I can make one up."

"Let us pray. 'In the name of the Father, the Son, and the Holy Spirit'," she began, and they all made the Sign of the Cross. "Dear God, please bless all the children in the First Communion class. Send the Holy Spirit to help them to open their hearts and their minds to You so that they will come to understand the Mystery of the Eucharist and the Holy Trinity. We ask this in the name of Jesus Christ, your Son. Amen."

"Now children, why don't you each say a special prayer to God?" urged Sister.

"Dear God, please make Danny's grandpa better," prayed Riley.

"God, please help us to learn our prayers and to solve the Mystery of the Eucharist," prayed Maria.

"Very nice," commented Sister Mary Rose in her softest voice.

They finished with the Sign of the Cross and then just sat for a while in front of the church. They listened to the sounds of the birds and the wind in the trees, and watched the people going by. Riley and Maria both felt very peaceful sitting there with Sister Mary Rose and thinking about God.

The children practiced their prayers at home with their families, at night before they went to bed, and especially in class with Deacon Paul and Ms. Kelly. They could recite from memory the prayers in the back of the book and were familiar with the prayers said out loud during Mass. When they were together, Riley and Maria always prayed the way that Sister Mary Rose had taught them and always asked God to please help them to solve the Mystery of the Eucharist.

CHAPTER 4
Come Sing to the Lord

The First Communion class had gathered for another Saturday morning lesson. Ms. Kelly was telling the children that in the next several weeks they would be learning more about the Mass and the Eucharist. In fact, Father Hugo would join them if his schedule allowed.

Suddenly organ music filled the church!

The children jumped up out of their seats. Startled, they looked to Ms. Kelly. She was looking up, over their heads. Their eyes followed her eyes. Then they saw, up in the choir loft, Sister Mary Rose seated at the huge organ, playing a loud, 'Alleluia' song. When she finished, the children clapped in delight. "Good morning class," she called from the choir loft.

"Good morning, Sister Mary Rose," they responded together.

"Children, you must know that music is a very important part of our worship of the Lord," said Ms. Kelly.

"I asked Sister Mary Rose if she would help us to learn to sing some of the hymns that will be sung during the Mass on your First Communion day. She thought it might be nice to begin by visiting the choir loft and taking a closer look at the pipe organ. What do you say?"

The children responded with excited 'yeahs', jumping at the occasion to see more of their church, especially that curious choir loft.

"Well, let's go," commanded Ms. Kelly as she led the procession of children down the church aisle and up the spiral staircase to the choir loft.

"Wow!" said Marisa as she looked over the rail to the church below. "The church looks even bigger and more beautiful from way up here." She reached out to take Nadine's hand to bring her friend closer to the rail. Marisa knew Nadine was afraid of heights and hoped that by taking her hand she would feel safe.

Enrico and Romano begged the children to come see the pipes that are part of the big pipe organ. They explained how the organ pushes air into and out of the pipes to make the sounds. Depending on the size of each pipe, a different sound comes out. The big pipes make real deep and rolling sounds. The thinner pipes make high and piercing sounds.

"Our mom and dad sing in the choir," said Romano. "Enrico and I sometimes come here with them on Sunday, but we have to stay out of the way and be very quiet. Mom says from here our voices can be heard all over the church."

"Indeed," commented Sister Mary Rose as the children gathered around her. "The church is designed so that from here, the sound of the pipe organ and the voices of the choir fill the church. We certainly do not want children's talking to fill the church, now do we?" she added with a wink of her eye.

"Did you know that music is an essential part of almost everything we do in church?" asked Sister Mary Rose. "We sing at Mass, we sing at weddings, we sing at funerals. We just love to sing to the Lord. St. Augustine taught us that 'he who sings prays twice'. That's because most of the songs or hymns sung in church are inspired by the Psalms or are prayers that saints and other devout people have written and that have been set to music."

"My Grandma's voice squeaks when she sings," said Erin. "Grandpa is even worse, he croaks like a frog," added her twin sister Bridget. "Should they be allowed to sing out loud in church like they do?" questioned Erin.

"Absolutely!" chuckled Sister Mary Rose. "Remember, God loves each and every one of us. During Mass, we should all sing to the Lord from our souls and with our very best voices, even if our voices are squeaky and croaky."

Sister passed out some papers and continued to talk. "There is certain music that we play and sing at Mass almost every Sunday. Other music and hymns change depending upon the season of the Church year and the occasion. On this paper you will find some of the special hymns that we will sing at the Mass for your First Communion. These hymns are also in the hymnals in the pews."

"Come, gather around the organ and we will practice singing the opening hymn. The first one on your sheet, *Gather Us In,* is the one that we will sing to begin Mass on your First Communion day. I will sing it through first so you get the tune. Then you sing with me."

They sang the hymn through three times. Ms. Kelly and Sister Mary Rose were delighted to hear that each time the little choir sounded better than the time before. As Sister explained the words, the hymn became more meaningful to the children.

"Very good, class," Sister Mary Rose complimented them. "Now, in the next few weeks, as you learn about the Mass, we will work on the other hymns. By First Communion Sunday these hymns and your voices will become part of the Mass."

"Thank you, Sister," called the children as they were led back down the spiral stairs. "That was fun, Sister. See you next week, Sister."

After class, Riley and Maria again sat in their favorite spot in front of the church to review what they had learned today about the Church and the Mystery of the Eucharist. They read aloud to each other the words of the hymns on the paper given to them by Sister Mary Rose. They noticed that many of the hymns were about bread and wine, the Lamb of God, and the Body and Blood of Christ. They read phrases like:

> *Here we will take the wine and the water,*
> *Here we will take the bread of new birth, . . .*

> *Lord God, Lamb of God,*
> *you take away the sins of the world: have mercy on us; . . .*

> *I want to walk as a child of the light.*
> *I want to follow Jesus.*
> *God set the stars to give light to the world.*
> *The star of my life is Jesus.*

> *I am the Bread of life.*
> *You who come to me shall not hunger. . .*

They realized that these hymns were leading them to solving the Mystery of the Eucharist. But the Mystery still remained a mystery!

CHAPTER 5
The Mass

Ms. Kelly was standing in front of the chalkboard in the parish hall classroom. "Today we are going to begin discussing the Mass," she said to the First Communion class. Next she took a piece of calk and divided the board into four big squares.

At the top of the first square she wrote 'Introductory Rite', on the next square she wrote 'Liturgy of the Word', the next was 'Liturgy of the Eucharist', and on the last square she wrote 'Concluding Rite'.

"I've seen most of you in church on Sunday with your families, so I am sure you are familiar with the Mass. I also know that the Mass can be confusing and a bit boring if you do not understand what is happening and how it all fits together. I thought it would be fun today if we could draw a picture of the Mass based on what you remember most from Sunday services.

"These four squares each represent a major part of the Mass. I want each of you to tell me your favorite part of the Mass. I will show you where it belongs and then we can talk about it. You can follow along from the PARTS OF THE MASS in the back of your books if you like."

With curious faces, the children gathered around.

"I like the story part best," volunteered Anthony with a chorus of "me too, me too, me too," sounded by Giancarlo, Andrew, and Mary Carol.

"Oh, this is a very important part of the Mass," said Ms. Kelly. "The story part, as you call it Anthony, is the main part of the Liturgy of the Word." In the square called Liturgy of the Word, Ms. Kelly wrote Old Testament Readings, the Psalms, Readings from the Acts and Letters of the Apostles, the Gospel and the Homily, and began to describe them.

"What does 'liturgy' mean?" interrupted T.J.

"Very good question, T.J. The Mass liturgy is the universal, authorized manner in which we Catholics come together and experience Jesus in scripture and in communion with one another," explained Ms. Kelly. "For example, it means that no matter where in the world the Mass is celebrated, it is always celebrated the same way. In a foreign

country you may not understand the language, but you will always know you are attending Mass because of the way in which it is celebrated. In fact, the order of the Mass we follow today was actually established by early Christians shortly after Jesus died and rose again. It has remained pretty much the same ever since."

"It is not really my favorite part," volunteered Yasmine, "but I want to know why you use that smelly, smoky stuff sometimes."

"That would be the incense. We often use it here, here, and here," said Ms. Kelly, pointing to the Introductory Rite, the Gospel, and Liturgy of the Eucharist. "You see, the rising smoke from the incense helps us to remember that we are part of the Communion of Saints. Our prayers go up to God in heaven and meet the prayers of saints who are already in heaven."

"That must be why my mommy says you can 'smell the saints praying' when you go to church," said Maria. She and Yasmine agreed that they really liked the smell of incense now.

"I like it when we all sing together in church," offered Giancarlo with a big grin.

"Singing is so much a part of the Mass, and I am so glad that you like it, Giancarlo. Sister Mary Rose is helping you with the music. Just look here and see how many times we sing during Mass," directed Ms. Kelly as she wrote the music titles in each of the squares.

"Praying out loud in church is fun," contributed Ryan. "It helps me to pay attention. Deacon Paul helped us practice saying the prayers said out loud during Mass. The two I remember are the Our Father and the Nicene Creed," added Ryan.

"Children, if you listen carefully, you will hear that in addition to the prayers that the entire congregation says together, the priest is constantly saying prayers during Mass. In fact, most of the Mass is prayer," concluded Ms. Kelly listing the prayers usually said at Mass.

"I like the Sign of Peace," said Anthony.

"My favorite is taking up the collection. My Grandpa Tim always gives me money to put in the collection basket," stated Matthew proudly.

Ms. Kelly asked the children to turn to the back of the books and read out loud what it says about Offering Gifts and the Sign of Peace.

As Ms. Kelly looked over the class she noticed that both Maria and Riley had been particularly quiet today. Then she noticed that they were once again whispering to each other. "So what's up with our two mystery solvers?" she said interrupting their whispering.

With a surprised look on his face, Riley offered, "Ms. Kelly, we want to know how come there isn't much written in the square for the Liturgy of the Eucharist? Why isn't it a favorite part? Is that because the Eucharist is still a mystery?" questioned Riley thinking he might be onto something.

"Well, I suppose that is part of it," responded Ms. Kelly. "But it is also probably not your favorite part of the Mass because, up until now, you have been too young to receive the Eucharist. That will change on your First Communion day."

Ms. Kelly noticed the children had become very quiet and seemed a bit 'starry-eyed'. After all, they had talked about a lot of very important things today. She decided it would be best to wait until next week to explain the Eucharist.

"Next week, children, I think Father Hugo will be with us and he will spend the entire class talking about and answering your questions on the Eucharist. How does that sound? In the meantime, pay particular attention during Mass tomorrow and see how much you remember from today's class. You might even take your books to church with you to follow along."

CHAPTER 6
The Story of the Eucharist

Father Hugo stood before a large painting and asked, "Who can tell me what this picture is about?"

"It's the Last Supper," replied Enrico. "We have a picture like it in our house."

"That is correct! Now, can you tell me what is happening here? Why is this such a famous picture? Who are these people?" Father continued to question.

"It's Jesus in the middle and these other guys are the Apostles," said Romano pointing to the men in the picture.

"Father, it looks like Jesus is saying Mass and giving Communion. See the chalice and the circle of bread in front of him. That's like what you do when you say Mass," observed Marisa.

"Brilliant observation!" commented Father Hugo. "You are all correct.

"This is a very famous picture. It is called The Last Supper. Many artists have painted different versions of this event, the Last Supper of Jesus. The most famous one was painted on a wall in Milano, Italy, by a man named Leonardo Da Vinci. The Da Vinci painting is now over 500 years old and people come from all over the world to see it. This picture of the Last Supper was painted in recent years by a very good friend of mine. My friend's name is Bill Shurtliff and he too is a famous artist."

"This picture shows Jesus with his twelve Apostles as they share the Passover meal on the night before Jesus was crucified. It was on this night that Jesus gave the Eucharist as a sacrament to the Apostles. He asked them to remember Him always by celebrating the Eucharist and sharing it with other people. So you are correct, Marisa, that is Jesus saying the very first Mass and giving the Apostles Communion.

"Months before this Last Supper, Jesus had explained to the Apostles that to have eternal life, which means to be with God forever, they would need to believe in Him, follow Him, and eat His Flesh and drink His Blood. Jesus said:

"Whoever eats my flesh and drinks my blood has eternal life, and I will raise him on the last day. For my flesh is true food, and my blood is true drink. Whoever eats my flesh and drinks my blood remains in me and I in him. Just as the living Father sent me and I have life because of the Father, so also the one who feeds on me will have life because of me. John 6:54-57

"At the Last Supper, Jesus was telling the Apostles that the bread He was holding in His hand and giving to them was His Body," Father said pointing to the picture. "He said that they should take it and eat it so that they could live with Him forever. He also was telling them that the wine was His Blood, and it would be shed for the forgiveness of their sins and

the sins of many. Later on He told the Apostles to *'do this in memory of me'* (Luke 22:19). This meant that the Apostles and the ordained priests who are the Apostles' successors should act in the person of Jesus to bring Christ to you in the Eucharist.

"Did they, do we, really eat flesh and drink blood?" asked Yasmine. "That sounds awful! I don't want to do that!"

"I know this is the hardest part to understand, children," Father Hugo began to explain. "Remember we talked a little about this when we were looking at the symbols of the lamb, wheat, and grapes in the windows of the church.

"You know that God can do anything and everything. At the Last Supper, and also when all the people of God are celebrating the Mass, Jesus is saying that these things that look like bread and wine actually become His Body and His Blood. God performs a miracle right before our very eyes. The bread and wine offered at the Last Supper and at our Mass really and truly become the Body, Blood, Soul, and Divinity of our Lord, Jesus Christ. We use a very big word to describe this. It is called 'transubstantiation'. The substance is truly Jesus; it just looks and tastes like bread and wine."

Father Hugo continued, "When you and I receive the Body and Blood of Jesus in Holy Communion, we receive special sacramental graces that help us to live our lives according to His rules. And, if we believe in Him, love our neighbors, and live our lives according to the Commandments, we will live forever with God in heaven."

The children sat quietly, thinking about what they had heard. Then Riley asked "Wasn't Jesus crucified the next day after this supper?"

"Yes He was," said Father Hugo. "During the Last Supper He was predicting His death, His sacrifice for the sake of the salvation of people everywhere, throughout time. Remember when we were looking at the stained glass windows and talked about the sacrifice of the lambs? Well, Jesus became the final, living sacrifice for the atonement of sins and protection from evil."

"So why did Jesus have to die and why was He tortured first? That's what these Stations of the Cross are about," said T.J. as he motioned to the Stations of the Cross.

"Very observant, T.J." Father explained. "When we make a sacrifice, we have to suffer somehow don't we? Otherwise it wouldn't be a sacrifice. What Jesus did was so tremendous and so good for us, that all the pain and suffering He went through was worth it to Him and to us. Jesus willingly endured the pain out of His love for us. Besides, He knew that He was going to rise up from being dead and would soon be in heaven with His Father. And He knew that He had shown all of us how we too can get to heaven and live eternally with Him, God the Father, and the Holy Spirit.

"Quite a set of miracles don't you think? Quite a mystery, too, wouldn't you say?" asked Father Hugo with a nod toward Maria and Riley.

Father Hugo noticed that both Maria and Riley had troubled expressions on their faces. Finally Riley asked, "Father, is it even possible to solve this mystery?"

Father, understanding his confusion, replied, "Children, remember how Maria's aunt explained the mysteries of the rosary. These mysteries are things that we would not ordinarily understand unless God revealed them to us. Well, that is true of the Mystery of the Eucharist. God has revealed the truth of the Eucharist to us through the Bible and Tradition. It is part of our faith."

Most children accepted what Father Hugo was saying. Only Maria and Riley still had doubts.

CHAPTER 7

Mystery Solved!

On the first Friday of every month, Maria and Riley went to church with their parents to attend Adoration of the Blessed Sacrament and Benediction. Up until today, it seemed to Maria and Riley that this was just something they did as families and friends, kind of like going to the movies together. But somehow today it was different.

Maria and Riley had only one more class left before making their First Communion on Sunday. Although Father Hugo, Ms. Kelly, and their parents had explained things over and over, they still felt frustrated and confused over the Mystery of the Eucharist and all the other 'mysteries' that had been talked about.

"Mommy says that during Adoration and Benediction Jesus is present on the altar in the Blessed Sacrament just the same as He is in Holy Communion. The Blessed Sacrament is the Eucharist," said Maria.

"I know," replied Riley. "My parents told me the same thing. The Host in the monstrance does look the same. My brain hurts from thinking about it so much; from trying to figure it all out; I mean solving the mysteries and all."

"I feel more troubled in here," said Maria pointing to where her heart lies. "Tonight let's pray that God will help us to understand."

Something came over Maria and Riley as they sat in the church with their families for Adoration of the Blessed Sacrament. The quiet of the church, the surroundings that had become so familiar, the smell of incense which remained, all reminded them of their Communion with the Saints. They sat quietly, patiently, comfortably, and happily before Jesus. They prayed silently, asking for His help.

That night, each in their own homes and in their own beds, Riley and Maria dreamed the same dream.

They were together in a place of light and fresh air and were dressed-up in their new clothes. In their midst was a man dressed in a white robe with sandals on his feet; he had rather long hair and a beard. It was Jesus!

Jesus beckoned them to sit down beside Him and rest. They were very sleepy. As they rested their heads on His knees, He spoke to them.

"My children, you work so hard to understand your faith and that pleases Me. Do not worry that you do not understand all things today. Remember that it is I who come to you when you come to Holy Communion. Receive Me, the Bread of Life, in Holy Communion. Keep the Commandments. Love your neighbor. Always put God first. Do these things and the Holy Spirit will bring you wisdom and understanding throughout your life, as you are ready. Your faith is your strength, let it be your guide."

The next morning, Riley and Maria could barely wait to tell each other about last night's dream. As they walked to the church for the last class before the big day, they talked and realized they both had the same dream. And together they came to the same realization. They had solved the mystery! They had to talk to Father Hugo right away.

"Father Hugo! Father Hugo!" they cried as they caught a glimpse of him in front of the church. "We figured it out!" they shouted.

"What is it Maria and Riley? You're early for class. What did you figure out?" Father Hugo responded, worried about their near panic condition.

"The mystery! We solved the mystery!" cried Maria and Riley together.

With a look of amazement, Father asked, "What on earth? How did you? Where did you? Well, what is the answer?"

"The mystery is our FAITH," beamed Maria. "We aren't sure what it is, but it is. It comes from God. It's His gift to us. It belongs to us forever. And it rests right in here," stated Maria pointing to where her heart lies.

"The more we study and the more we pray, the bigger it gets," contributed Riley. "The grace we will receive from Holy Communion will

make our faith grow bigger and better. The Holy Spirit will see to that!

"It's okay that we haven't solved the entire Mystery of the Eucharist by now. Jesus told us that as our faith grows, we will understand more-and-more about Him and the Mysteries. We just need to keep praying and listening."

"That is absolutely right," said Father Hugo, with a hint of a tear in his eye. "I am so proud of both of you. Truly you are ready to receive your First Holy Communion tomorrow. Come let's share this with Ms. Kelly and the other children and say a prayer of thanks to God for giving you these gifts."

CHAPTER 8
First Communion Day

At last! The day to receive their First Holy Communion had arrived. The girls in their beautiful white dresses and veils, and boys in their handsome suits, white shirts, and ties, were gathering in the vestibule of the church. The parents, family members, and other parishioners were being seated. The sanctuary had been decorated with beautiful white flowers: lilies, roses, mums, and carnations. The church looked like heaven on earth.

Father Hugo and Deacon Paul had on their Mass vestments and were greeting people at the door as they arrived. Sister Mary Rose was there too, dressed in her beautiful white habit for this special occasion. Ms. Kelly fussed over the children making sure the veils were on straight and the ties tied right. She felt as though her heart might burst out of love for these special boys and girls. As the bell in the tower above the church began to toll out the hour, Sister hurried up the stairs to the choir loft where the full church choir was waiting. The children lined up as they had practiced the day before. They were to lead the procession to begin Mass. They would be followed by the altar servers, the readers, Deacon Paul, and finally Father Hugo.

On cue, the music began and the choir, the children, and everyone in the church began to sing the entrance hymn:

Here in this place, new light is streaming,
Now is the darkness vanished away,
See in this space our fears and our dreamings,
Brought here to you in the light of this day.

From 'Gather Us In'
Text by Marty Haugen

The children filed in as planned and took their places at the ends of the pews in the front of the church beside their families.

Father Hugo and Deacon Paul ascended the steps, turned and kissed the altar, and Mass began.

The children followed the Mass with complete attention. Their voices blended in with the choir and the other parishioners in song and prayer. They were now very much a part of the Church community.

When it came time for Communion, one by one, each child, accompanied by his or her family, approached the altar and Father Hugo to receive the Eucharist. The Body and Blood of Jesus Christ. Their First Holy Communion.

When it was Riley's turn to receive Communion, he looked around and found his best friend, Maria next to him. They smiled at each other, their eyes bright with newly found knowledge. They had solved the mystery together and together they were entering into another phase of their lives. There would be more mysteries to come, but with their faith and their friendship Riley felt they could face anything together. He took Maria's hand and they walked up to Father Hugo side by side to receive their First Holy Communion.

After Mass was ended, all the children gathered for pictures. First they were around the altar. Then they went to the baptism font which is the place where it all began: the place where they received their first Sacrament, Baptism, and became members of the Body of Christ and of His Church.

"Why is this such a special day?" quizzed Father Hugo.

Together, the children shouted back, each answering for themselves,

"Because, Today I Made My First Communion!"

THE END

Look in the Back of the Book

Map of Our Church

Prayers I Should Know

The Rosary

The Commandments

Parts of the Mass

Map of Our Church

1 Altar
2 Ambo
3 Ambry
4 Baptismal font
5 Candles

6 Choir
7 Choir loft
8 Crucifix
9 Holy water font
10 Monstrance

11 Organ and other musical instruments
12 Reconciliation room
13 Sacristy
14 Sanctuary
15 Stained glass windows
16 Stations of the cross
17 Statues
18 Tabernacle

Map of Our Church (Definitions)

1 ALTAR   The raised area in the center of the sanctuary where the priest presides at Mass and consecrates the bread and wine into the Body and Blood of Christ. The area is raised to signify its importance. The altar represents Christ, the Head of the Church, in His heavenly realm while the worshipers, the Body of the Church, are in the earthly realm.

2 AMBO   The stand beside the altar from which the Liturgy of the Word is celebrated. Some people call it a pulpit. From here, the priest, deacon, and specially trained lay parishioners read from the Old Testament, the New Testament, and the Gospel. This is also where the priest or deacon usually delivers his homily.

3 AMBRY   The cabinet in the sanctuary or baptistery area that contains the holy oils that are used in the Sacraments throughout the year. The holy oils, also called chrisms, are blessed by the Bishop on Holy Thursday and carried that day to all the churches in the diocese.

4 BAPTISMAL FONT   The big font filled with water and used when babies or other people are baptized into the Church. Usually the baby is held over the water as the priest or deacon pours water over the baby's forehead as he says, "I baptize you in the name of the Father, of the Son, and of the Holy Spirit."

In some churches the font is very big so that if the parents want, the baby can be baptized by immersion in the water.

If people are too big to be held over the font, the priest or deacon takes water out of the font, has them stand next to it, and then pours the water over their heads.

5 CANDLES   The candle flame represents the presence of God, who gives light to us and who enlightens us by His word. A candle always burns before the Real Presence in the Eucharist. Candles are lit during mass. Sometimes small votive or vigil candles are placed before statues to accompany prayer intentions and requests.

6 CHOIR   The group of people who sing during the Mass and who lead the congregation in singing hymns.

7 CHOIR LOFT   The area from which the choir sings. In our church it is an open loft area above the body of the church. Choir lofts are designed so that the sounds of the organ and choir resonate out into the body of the church.

8 CRUCIFIX   The cross bearing the figure of Christ crucified. A representation of the crucified Jesus must be on or over the altar where and when Mass is celebrated.

9 HOLY WATER FONT   Holy water fonts are placed at the entrances of the church. As we enter and leave the church we dip the fingers of our right hand in the holy water, then make the Sign of the Cross. The intention is the remembrance and reconfirmation of our Baptism vows.

10 MONSTRANCE   The ornamental stand that holds the Eucharist/Blessed Sacrament during Adoration and Benediction. In the center is a clear glass cylinder that holds the Eucharist. Often around the cylinder are rays of gold that look like rays of light. Jesus is the Light of the world. The rays also show our faith bursting out from the Light. The cylinder is elevated on a stand. The stand not only helps us to see the light, but also represents our hope in reaching God in Heaven.

11 ORGAN AND OTHER MUSICAL INSTRUMENTS   The principal source of music used in our church is the pipe organ. It is located in the choir loft. The pipe organ is the traditional musical instrument used in Catholic churches. Sometimes, on special occasions, our church has an entire orchestra play music for the Mass. Other times, especially when the children's choir sings, we use a piano, flute, and/or guitar.

12 RECONCILIATION ROOM (also called the Confessional) The small room where the Sacrament of Penance and Reconciliation takes place. It is designed so that we poor sinners can sit with the priest who represents Jesus, confess our sins, obtain advice on how to improve our lives, receive our penance, and be absolved of our sins. Usually we must leave the room to complete our penance, usually prayers or good deeds. We have to complete our penance to become fully reconciled in the good graces of the Lord.

13 SACRISTY   The area behind the sanctuary. This is the area where the priest, deacon, and altar servers put on their vestments before Mass. It is also where the chalices and ciborium used during Mass may be purified. The area has a special sink used to purify items that come in contact with the Eucharist. This sink drains into the ground to prevent any part of the Eucharist from entering into the municipal water system.

14 SANCTUARY   The entire area in the front and center of the church. This is the area where the Mass is celebrated. It contains the altar, the ambo, chairs for the priest, deacon, any visiting priests,

the bishop when he visits, and the altar servers. The crucifix is located in the center of the sanctuary.

15 STAINED GLASS WINDOWS The windows of churches can be made of colorful stained glass with intricate patterns that illustrate biblical stories and/or images of Jesus, Mary, the Apostles, Saints, and symbols of faith and Christianity.

16 STATIONS OF THE CROSS Pictures and/or carvings that depict the story of how Jesus was condemned to die, suffered, was nailed to the Cross, died and was buried. Then He arose from the dead on Easter morning, proving to all that He truly is the Son of God.

17 STATUES   Most churches have statues of Mary, Joseph, baby Jesus, and other saints to remind us of the service and sacrifice that these great saints made to spread the faith. The statues are also there to remind us to pray to the saints for their intercession on our behalf and in our prayers to God.

18 TABERNACLE   The special container where the unconsumed, consecrated bread, the Body of Christ, is kept after Communion. The Eucharist is held in the tabernacle until a priest, deacon, or lay minister takes it to parish members who are in nursing homes, hospitals, or who cannot come to Mass because they are sick or until it is given in Holy Communion at a later service. The tabernacle is always located in a prominent location near the altar. Parishioners are welcome to kneel or sit before the tabernacle in adoration of the Blessed Sacrament, the Eucharist.

Prayers I Should Know

SIGN OF THE CROSS

In the name of the Father, and of the Son, and of the Holy Spirit. Amen

OUR FATHER

Our Father, who art in heaven, hallowed be Thy name; Thy kingdom come; Thy will be done on earth as it is in heaven. Give us this day our daily bread; and forgive us our trespasses as we forgive those who trespass against us; and lead us not into temptation, but deliver us from evil. Amen.

HAIL MARY

Hail Mary, full of grace! The Lord is with thee; blessed art thou among women, and blessed is the fruit of thy womb, Jesus.

Holy Mary, Mother of God, pray for us sinners, now and at the hour of our death. Amen.

APOSTLES' CREED

(Note: Tradition tells us that the Apostles would have used this Creed to tell people what they believe. It is nice for us to say when we want to remind ourselves or tell other people what 'I believe'.)

I believe in God, the Father almighty, Creator of heaven and earth, and in Jesus Christ, his only Son our Lord, who was conceived by the Holy Spirit, born of the Virgin Mary, suffered under Pontius Pilate, was crucified, died and was buried; he descended into hell; on the third day he rose again from the dead; he ascended into heaven, and is seated at the right hand of God the Father almighty; from there he will come to judge the living and the dead. / I believe in the Holy Spirit, the holy catholic Church, the communion of saints, the forgiveness of sins, the resurrection of the body, and life everlasting. Amen.

NICENE CREED

(Note: The Nicene Creed is used during most Masses to profess our faith. It was made part of the Liturgy of the Eucharist in the fourth Century and received it's name from the Council of Nicene held in 325 A.D.)

I believe in one God, the Father almighty, maker of heaven and earth, of all things visible and invisible. / I believe in one Lord Jesus Christ, the Only Begotten Son of God, born of the Father before all ages. God from God, Light from Light, true God from true

God, begotten, not made, consubstantial with the Father; through him all things were made. For us men and for our salvation he came down from heaven and by the Holy Spirit was incarnate of the Virgin Mary, and became man. / For our sake he was crucified under Pontius Pilate, he suffered death and was buried, and rose again on the third day in accordance with the Scriptures. He ascended into heaven and is seated at the right hand of the Father. He will come again in glory to judge the living and the dead and his kingdom will have no end. / I believe in the Holy Spirit, the Lord, the giver of life, who proceeds from the Father and the Son, who with the Father and the Son is adored and glorified, who has spoken through the prophets. I believe in one, holy, catholic, and apostolic Church. I confess one Baptism for the forgiveness of sins and I look forward to the resurrection of the dead and the life of the world to come. Amen.

GLORY BE

Glory be to the Father, and to the Son, and to the Holy Spirit. As it was in the beginning, is now, and ever shall be, world without end. Amen.

PRAYER TO THE HOLY SPIRIT

O Holy Spirit, Eternal God with the Father and Son, who sees all my actions and counts all my steps, from whom no thought is hidden, enlighten me that I may clearly see what evil I have done today, and what good I have left undone. And move my heart that I may sincerely repent and amend my life. Amen.

ACT OF CONTRITION (VERSION 1)

O my God, I am heartily sorry for having offended You, and I detest all my sins, because I dread the loss of heaven and the pains of hell, but most of all because they offend You, my God, who are good and deserving of all my love. I firmly resolve, with the help of Your grace, to confess my sins, to do penance and to amend my life. Amen.

ACT OF CONTRITION (VERSION 2)

My God, I am sorry for my sins with all my heart.
In choosing to do wrong and failing to do good, I have sinned against You whom I should love above all things. I firmly intend with Your help, to do penance, to sin no more, and to avoid whatever leads me to sin.

PRAYER TO ST. MICHAEL

St. Michael the Archangel, defend us in battle. Be our protection against the wickedness and snares of the devil. May God rebuke him, we humbly pray, and do thou, O Prince of the heavenly host, by the power of God, cast into hell Satan and all the evil spirits who prowl throughout the world seeking the ruin of souls. Amen.

PRAYER TO ONE'S GUARDIAN ANGEL

Angel of God, my guardian dear, to whom God's love commits me here, ever this day (night) be at my side, to light and guard, to rule and guide. Amen.

The Rosary

The Rosary is a prayer that helps us to remember events in the life of Jesus Christ, his mother, Mary, and the history of our salvation. Praying the Rosary and meditating on the mysteries helps us to better understand our faith and to give glory to God.

There are four parts to the Rosary. The first three parts gradually took form during the second millennium, that is the second 1,000 years following Christ's birth. These first three parts ask us to reflect on the joyful, sorrowful, and glorious events in the life of Jesus and His Mother. On October 16, 2002, Pope John Paul II, suggested adding a forth part to the Rosary. This part is to reflect on Jesus' public life and is called the mysteries of light, or the luminous mysteries.

Depending on the day of the week, a different part of the Rosary is prayed. Pope John Paul II recommends saying the luminous mysteries on Thursday. On Monday and Saturday, the part we say reflects on the joyful mysteries (or events). On Tuesday and Friday we pray the sorrowful mysteries, and on Wednesday and Sunday we usually pray the glorious mysteries. However, on Sundays from Advent to Lent we pray the joyful mysteries; during Lent we pray the sorrowful mysteries; from Easter to Advent we pray the glorious mysteries.

To begin praying the Rosary, we make the Sign of the Cross, recite the Apostles' Creed, an Our Father, and three Hail Mary's.

For each mystery, we think deeply about the event. What was Jesus doing? What was Mary doing? How does that event affect our life? Then we recite a set of prayers for each mystery:

- One Our Father
- Ten Hail Marys
- The Glory Be to the Father

After the last mystery of the Rosary we pray the Hail Holy Queen prayer. We end the Rosary with the Sign of the Cross.

The four parts of the Rosary and the mysteries are:

THE JOYFUL MYSTERIES

1. The Annunciation. The Archangel Gabriel, a messenger from God, announces to Mary that she is to be the Mother of God.
2. The Visitation. Mary visits and helps her cousin Elizabeth, who is also soon to become a mother. Elizabeth's baby will grow up to be John the Baptist.
3. The Nativity. Mary gives birth to Jesus in a stable in Bethlehem.
4. The Presentation. Jesus, the baby, is presented to God in the Jewish temple in observance of the Law of Moses.

5. The Finding of Jesus in the Temple. The boy Jesus, whom His parents thought was lost, is found in the temple teaching and learning from the doctors.

THE SORROWFUL MYSTERIES

1. The Agony in the Garden. Jesus goes to the garden to pray and is overcome with great sorrow and anguish because of the sins of mankind.
2. The Scourging at the Pillar. Jesus is falsely accused, insulted, and scourged (beaten with whips).
3. Crowning with Thorns. The Jews and Romans mock and humiliate Jesus about being the "king of the Jews" and they place a crude crown made of thorns on His head.
4. The Carrying of the Cross. Jesus is condemned to death and then forced to carry the cross on which He will be crucified through the streets of Jerusalem.
5. The Crucifixion. Jesus is crucified and dies on the cross for our sins.

THE GLORIOUS MYSTERIES

1. The Resurrection. After Jesus dies on the cross, He is placed in a burial tomb. Three days later He arises from the dead and appears to His Apostles.
2. The Ascension. Jesus ascends into heaven and takes His place at the right hand of the Father.
3. The Descent of the Holy Spirit. The Holy Spirit descends on the Apostles and Mary and enlightens them to spread the Gospel.
4. The Assumption. Mary, who was born free of original sin and remained free of sin throughout her life, is consumed by divine love and is taken up to heaven to be with Jesus.
5. The Coronation. Mary is crowned queen of heaven, all the angels and saints, and of all the earth.

THE LUMINOUS MYSTERIES

1. The Baptism of Jesus in the Jordan. As Jesus, in obedience to the Father, descends into the water, the heavens open wide and the voice of the Father declares Him the beloved Son, while the Holy Spirit descends on Him to invest Him with the mission He is to carry out.
2. The Wedding Feast at Cana. Jesus, in this first public sign, changes water into wine and opens the hearts of the disciples to faith.
3. The Proclamation of the Kingdom of God. Jesus proclaims the Kingdom of God and calls to conversion and the forgiveness of sins those who draw near to Him in humble trust; through His mercy He provided for us the Sacrament of Reconciliation.
4. The Transfiguration. The glory of the Godhead shines forth from the face of Christ as the Father commands the Apostles to 'listen to Him' and prepare to experience with Him the agony of the Passion, so as to come with Him to the joy of the Resurrection and a life transfigured by the Holy Spirit.
5. The Institution of the Eucharist. Jesus offers his body and blood as food under the signs of bread and wine during the Last Supper and testifies His love for humanity 'to the end' by offering Himself in sacrifice for our salvation.

The Commandments

THE TEN COMMANDMENTS

I am the LORD your God: you shall not have strange gods before Me.

You shall not take the name of the LORD your God in vain.

Remember to keep holy the LORD's Day.

Honor your father and your mother.

You shall not kill.

You shall not commit adultery.

You shall not steal.

You shall not bear false witness against your neighbor.

You shall not covet your neighbor's wife.

You shall not covet your neighbor's goods.

THE GREATEST COMMANDMENTS

When the Apostles asked Jesus what was the greatest commandment, He responded saying:

"You shall love the Lord, your God, with all your heart, with all your soul, and with all your mind. This is the greatest and the first commandment. The second is like it: You shall love your neighbor as yourself." Matthew 22:37–39

Jesus is saying that loving and honoring God, as established in the first three commandments, are the most important things in our entire lives. The other seven commandments proclaim how we should love our neighbor, our fellow man, and ourselves.

Parts of the Mass

INTRODUCTORY RITE

Entrance Hymn/Chant

We begin the Holy Sacrifice of the Mass by lifting our hearts and voices to God, telling Him how glad we are to be here and that we are ready to welcome Him into our hearts, to listen to His word, and to receive Him in the Eucharist.

Greeting and Entrance Antiphon

The priest kisses (an act of veneration) the altar and leads the congregation in the Sign of the Cross. He begins the Mass with an opening prayer.

Penitential Rite

The priest asks us to recall our sins and to tell God how terribly sorry we are for having offended Him. We lay our sins at the foot of the cross, where Jesus was sacrificed for the forgiveness of our sins.

Together we recite the prayer of repentance. Then we ask God to have mercy on us.

We say or sing in English, *or* We say or sing in the original Greek:

Lord, have mercy.	*Kyrie Eleison.*
Christ, have mercy.	*Christe Eleison.*
Lord, have mercy.	*Kyrie Eleison.*

The Greek helps us to realize that the Mass is very old and universal.

Gloria

The Gloria is sung in praise of God and to give thanks to God. On Sundays in the Easter season, the priest will go throughout the church to sprinkle the congregation with holy water. This invites all present to renew their baptismal vow by making the Sign of the Cross.

Opening Prayer/Collect

The priest recites an opening prayer to God, our Father, to help us to open our hearts and minds to the Lord and to help us to live our lives according to His will.

Incense of Altar, Ambo, and Congregation

Sometimes the priest or deacon will circle the altar with incense during the Introductory Rite. Incense is a substance of spices, gums, and resins. When set afire it gives off a perfumed smoke. It was an ancient Jewish tradition to place incense in golden cups and burn it during religious services. The Book of Revelation in the Bible refers to the golden bowls of incense that give rise to the prayers of the saints. During Mass it helps us to remember that we are part of the Communion of Saints, and our prayers raise to God along with the prayers of saints who have gone on to heaven before us.

LITURGY OF THE WORD

First Reading

The first reading is from the Old Testament of the Bible (except during the Easter season). The Old Testament tells of how God spoke to man through the Prophets and its stories prefigure the coming of the Messiah, Jesus Christ.

Responsorial Psalm

The Psalms are part of the Old Testament of the Bible and include songs or hymns of praise, thanksgiving, and calls for help and/or instruction on how to follow the commandments.

Second Reading

This reading is generally taken from the Letters of the Apostles found in the New Testament. The Apostles wrote these letters to instruct new Christians and to convert others to Christianity.

Alleluia or Gospel Acclamation

Before the Gospel is read, the Alleluia is sung or read (except during Lent). Alleluia means "praise the Lord" in Hebrew.

Gospel

The third reading comes from the part of the New Testament that is called the Gospel. There are four books to the Gospel, one each written by Matthew, Mark, Luke, and John. The Gospel books are direct accounts of the life and works of Jesus Christ, His death on the cross, and His resurrection from the dead. They are very, very important; that's why we stand to hear readings from them. Only the priest or the deacon is allowed to read the Gospel during Mass. Sometimes the priest or deacon will incense the book of Gospels before reading from it.

Homily

Following the Gospel reading, either the priest or deacon delivers a talk called a Homily. The Homily is intended to make a connection between what we learn from the readings and how we should live our lives. The Homily also prepares us for receiving the Eucharist.

Profession of Faith, the Creed

The entire congregation recites or sings the Creed out loud. The Creed puts into words what we as Christians believe about God, the Trinity, how we got here, and where we are going. Most of the time the Nicene Creed is used; however, particularly during Lent and Easter, the Apostles' Creed may be used instead.

General Intercessions- Prayers of the Faithful

At this point, we stop and pray for the Pope and all the Bishops and clergy, for the health and welfare of our country, those who lead us, those who protect us, for the sick and disabled, for the less fortunate, for peoples throughout the world, and for other special intentions of the community and congregation on this day.

LITURGY OF THE EUCHARIST

Preparation of the Altar

The Liturgy of the Eucharist is a recurrence of the events of the Last Supper, Jesus' sacrifice for our salvation, and His resurrection. Before this begins, the priest has to prepare the table for supper, i.e., the altar for the Eucharistic banquet. The altar servers assist the priest by bringing the empty chalices, the ciborium, and the altar cloths.

Offering of Gifts

When we go to someone's home for a banquet, we bring gifts. The same thing happens when we go to Mass; people bring gifts. The ushers take up the collection in which people put money to operate the church and help the poor. Sometimes people bring gifts of food and other things for those in need and place them in a box by the front door. The money and food are not only gifts, but they represent a sacrifice. This money and food could be used by our families, but instead we sacrifice them to help the Church to do God's work.

Always on Sunday a few people are asked to carry bread (or hosts) and wine to the altar. This represents the gifts of the entire church community, including the gift from those people who may not have any other gift to offer this day.

During the Offering of Gifts we also make spiritual sacrifices to God.

Presentation Hymn

As the altar is prepared, collection taken up, and gifts presented, the congregation sings a hymn to offer our hearts to God.

Prayer Over the Gifts

The priest prays that our gifts and sacrifices will be acceptable to God.

Eucharistic Prayer

The Eucharistic Prayer begins somewhat like our prayer before meals. We praise God and thank Him for all our blessings and most especially we thank Him for sending Jesus to save us from death. We say and do "lift our hearts up to the Lord."

Our gifts of bread and wine become the Body and Blood of Christ

The priest re-presents the sacrifice of Jesus by consecrating the bread and wine on the altar into the Body and Blood of Christ. This happens when the priest first holds up the bread and says:

> Before He was given up to death, a death He freely accepted, He took bread and gave you thanks. He broke the bread, gave it to His disciples, and said: Take this all of you, and eat it: this is My Body which will be given up for you

Then the priest takes the chalice with the wine in it and says:

> When supper was ended, He took the cup. Again He gave you thanks and praise, and gave the cup to His disciples, and said: Take this, all of you, and drink from it: this is the cup of My Blood, the Blood of the new and everlasting covenant. It will be shed for you and for all so that sins may be forgiven. Do this in memory of Me.

A miracle happens. The miracle is the transubstantiation of the bread and wine into the Body, Blood, Soul, and Divinity of Jesus Christ. The miracle is the Mystery of the Eucharist!

Memorial Acclamation

The entire congregation acknowledges their faith by acclaiming out loud their belief in Jesus' sacrifice, resurrection, and promise to come again at the end of the world. The most common one used is *We proclaim your Death, or Lord, and profess your Resurrection until you come again.*

Lord's Prayer

We recite the Lord's Prayer and by doing so acknowledge God as the Almighty and to ask Him to make us more like Him.

Sign of Peace

The priest offers all the promise of peace and unity with Jesus in Heaven. The congregation then may offer each other a sign of peace. This allows us to make peace with our neighbors and forgive them their trespasses so that our souls are ready to receive Jesus in the Eucharist. It's sort of like getting ready for Heaven here on earth.

Reception of Communion

Before the priest or lay minister distributes Communion, the priest recalls that Jesus is the sacrificial lamb, breaks the bread, and prays:

> Lamb of God, you take away the sins of the world, have mercy on us.
> Lamb of God, you take away the sins of the world, have mercy on us.
> Lamb of God, you take away the sins of the world, grant us peace.

Then all present, who have made or are making their First Communion, have fasted for at least one hour before, and are in a state of Grace (that is free from mortal sin), may receive the Eucharist in Holy Communion with the Church.

As Communion is distributed, they proclaim to each person, The Body of Christ, and The Blood of Christ. The person receiving the Body and Blood responds, Amen. That means "so be it" or "I believe."

Communion Hymn

The choir and congregation sing a song during Communion. This tells God how very happy we are to be able to receive Him.

Prayer After Communion

After a period of silence, during which we should be thanking God for His generosity and this wonderful opportunity, the priest reads an after communion prayer.

CONCLUDING RITES

Blessing

After the announcements are read, the priest blesses the congregation and all make the Sign of the Cross together.

Dismissal

The priest tells everyone, *Go forth, the Mass is ended.*

Closing Hymn

The closing hymn provides a sung prayer of thanksgiving and lets us leave the church with joy in our hearts.

Memories of My First Communion Day

About Today

My name is:

Today is:

The church where I made my First Communion is:

The priest who said Mass for my First Communion is:

Friends and relatives who helped me celebrate my First Communion are:

This is what we did to celebrate:

My Favorite Things

(Describe or draw a picture of your favorite things)

My favorite part of the Mass is:

My favorite part of the church is:

My favorite prayer is:

My favorite song or hymn is:

Why the Eucharist Is Important to Me

These Are My Teachers and My Classmates

Pictures & Memories

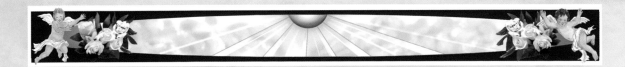

Pictures & Memories

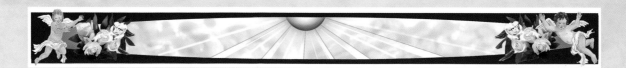